A Visit to
INDIA

Peter & Connie Roop

Heinemann Library
Des Plaines, Illinois

© 1998 Reed Educational & Professional Publishing
Published by Heinemann Library,
an imprint of Reed Educational & Professional Publishing,
1350 East Touhy Avenue, Suite 240 West
Des Plaines, IL 60018

Designed by AMR
Illustrations by Art Construction
Printed in Hong Kong / China

02 01 00
10 9 8 7 6 5 4 3 2

Library of Congress Cataloging-in-Publication Data

Roop, Peter.
    India / Peter & Connie Roop.
        p.   cm. -- (A visit to)
    Includes index.
    Summary: Introduces the country of India, including the land, landmarks, homes, food, clothes, work, transportation, language, school, sports, celebrations, and the arts.
    ISBN 1-57572-710-2 (library binding)
    1. India--Juvenile literature. [1. India.] I. Roop, Connie.
II. Title. III. Series. IV. Series: Roop, Peter. Visit to.
    DS407.R62   1998
    954--dc21
                                                        98-12451
                                                            CIP
                                                            AC

Acknowledgments
The Publishers would like to thank the following for permission to reproduce photographs:
J. Allan Cash: pp. 7, 8, 14, 15, 18, 21, 28, 29; Hutchison Library: J. Horner pp. 10, 23, J. Highet p. 25, L. Taylor p. 22; Images of India: pp. 13, 27; Magnum: R. Raghu pp.19, 24; Panos Pictures: S. Anwar p. 6, R. Berriedale-Johnson p. 5, N. Durrell-McKenna p. 12, J Horner p. 16, Z Nelson p. 11, D O'Leary pp. 17, 20, P. Smith pp. 9, 26

Cover photograph reproduced with permission of Spectrum Color Library

Every effort has been made to contact copyright holders of any material reproduced in this book. Any omissions will be rectified in subsequent printings if notice is given to the Publisher.

Any words appearing in bold, **like this**, are explained in the Glossary.

Contents

India

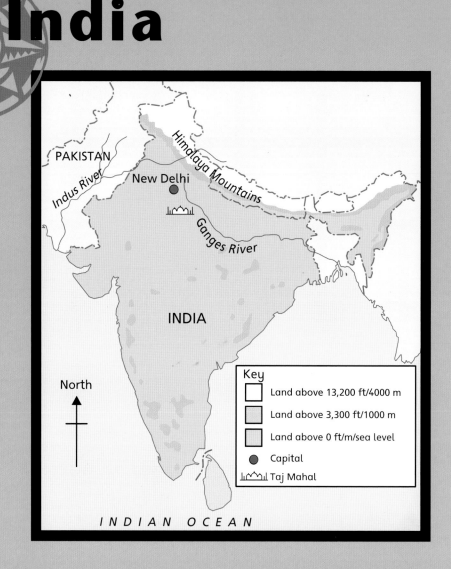

PAKISTAN

Himalaya Mountains

Indus River

New Delhi

Ganges River

INDIA

North

Key
- Land above 13,200 ft/4000 m
- Land above 3,300 ft/1000 m
- Land above 0 ft/m/sea level
- ● Capital
- Taj Mahal

INDIAN OCEAN

India is in Asia. It is shaped like a diamond. India takes its name from the Indus River. This river runs through Pakistan, which used to be part of India.

Many people live in India. Only China has more people than India. Indians eat, sleep, play, and go to school like you. Life in India is also **unique**.

Land

India has three main types of land. In the north of the country are the Himalaya Mountains. These are the highest mountains in the world.

The middle of India forms the largest **plain** in the world. The other part of India is a **peninsula**. It has high, flat mountains and many miles of beautiful seashore.

Landmarks

The Taj Mahal is India's most famous
building. It was built 300 years ago
in memory of a much-loved queen,
named Mumtaz Mahal.

The Ganges River is a long, wide river.
To many Indians, it is a holy river.
People pray and wash along the banks
of the Ganges River.

Homes

In the cities, people live in small apartments. Many poor people live in huts or tents or have no homes at all. It is very dangerous for these people during the **monsoon season.**

Most people live in country villages.
Some homes are made of **bamboo** or
homemade clay bricks. Many large
families live together in one building.

Food

Many Indians eat only vegetables and seafood, which are cooked with fresh spices. Rice or bread is served with every meal. Indian breads are round and flat.

A popular dish is *tandoori* (tan-DOH-ree), which is meat cooked in a very hot, clay oven. Another favorite meal is *dhal* (DALL), a thick soup eaten with bread.

13

Clothes

Most Indian women wear **saris**. They are
cool and comfortable. They can be very
plain for work, or **embroidered** in
beautiful colors for special days.

Some men wear loose pants called *pajamas.* Farmers wear *dhotis* (DOH-tees), which are cloths tied around their waist. In the cities, many people wear clothes like yours.

15

Work

Most Indians are farmers. They grow
rice, tea, sugarcane, wheat, fruit, and
vegetables. They can grow two **crops**
a year in the hot, wet weather.

Some people work in **factories** and make
cloth, computers, bicycles, cars, and tools.
Many people make and sell things from
their own home.

Transportation

In the crowded streets, you will see trucks, cars, bicycles, rickshaws (three-wheeled bicycles for people or heavy loads), and people walking.

Most trains and buses are so full that people ride on the roof. India's rivers are also very busy. Large and small boats carry people and **cargo**.

Language

There are many different groups of Indian people. Each group has its own **customs** and beliefs. More than 75 languages are spoken in India.

Hindi is the most important language
in India. Hindi and English are taught
in schools so that all Indians can speak
to each other.

School

Children go to school from ages six to fourteen. They study Hindi, English, math, history, and geography.

Many children are too poor to go to school. Their families need them to stay at home. The children help farm or they beg in the streets.

Free Time

Many Indians enjoy a sport called cricket. Children practice on the streets with a bat and ball. Other popular sports are field hockey, badminton, polo, and soccer.

Movies are very popular in India. Indian movie stars are treated like heroes. Families also enjoy amusement parks in the early evening.

Celebrations

Each **religion** in India has many festivals. *Diwali* (di-WALL-ee) is the Hindu New Year. It lasts for five days. Many lamps and fireworks make it a festival of light.

Hindus also believe that cows are holy. The festival of *Pongal* honors them. The cows are washed, painted, and decorated with flowers.

The Arts

Many Indians enjoy making crafts from metal, wood, stone, or cloth. They use bright colors and detailed patterns in their paintings and clothes.

The sitar is a famous Indian instrument.
It is like a guitar that has up to 26 strings.
Sometimes people dance to sitar music.
These dances often tell old stories.

Fact File

Name	The full name of India is the Republic of India.
Capital	The **capital** of India is New Delhi.
Language	Most Indians speak Hindi and some English, but there are 75 other languages spoken in India.
Population	There are about 950 million people living in India.
Money	Instead of the dollar, the Indians have the *rupee* (ROO-pee).
Religion	Most Indians believe in Hinduism, which worships many gods. As well as Hindus, there are also some Muslims, Christians, and Sikhs.
Products	India produces lots of rice, wheat, tea, sugar, coffee, jewelry, clothes and machines.

Words You Can Learn

ek (ik)	one
do (daw)	two
tin (dean)	three
namaste (nahm-as-teh)	hello
namaste	goodbye
shukrinya	thank you
mehabani seh (meha-bani seh)	please

Glossary

bamboo	a tall plant with a long, strong stem
capital	the city where the government is based
cargo	things that are transported
crops	plants that are grown and harvested
customs	the way people do things
embroidered	stitches used to decorate material
factories	places where many of the same things are made
lentil	a kind of bean
monsoon season	a time of very rainy weather
peninsula	land with water on three sides
plain	an area of open, flat land
religions	what people believe in
saris	long pieces of cloth wrapped around the waist and shoulders
unique	different in a special way

Index

More Books to Read

Dahl, Michael. *India*. Danbury, CT: Children's Press. 1997.

Das, Pordeepta. *I is for India*. Morristown, NJ: Silver Burdett Press. 1996.

Streissguth, Thomas. *India*. Minneapolis, MN: The Lerner Publishing Group. 1998.